TWELVE
MONTHS
GARDEN
ORGANISER

TWELVE MONTHS GARDEN ORGANISER

by H. G. Witham Fogg

Edited by Jim Mather

foulsham

LONDON • NEW YORK • TORONTO • SYDNEY

foulsham

Yeovil Road, Slough, Berkshire SL1 4JH

ISBN 0–572–01641–7
Copyright © 1991 W. Foulsham and Co. Ltd

Printed in Great Britain at
St. Edmundsbury Press,
Bury St. Edmunds.

Contents

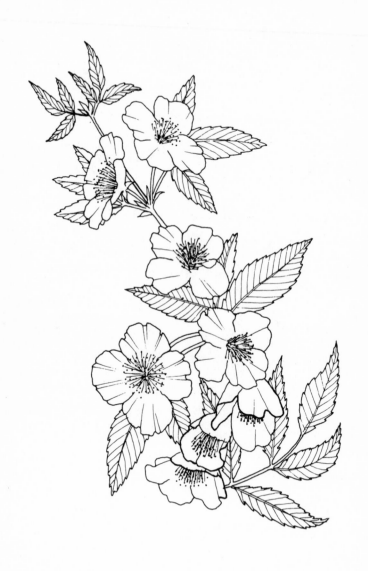

CHAPTER ONE

The Secrets of Good Timing

What can I be doing in the garden now? This is one of the eternal questions asked by every enthusiast. Sometimes the question changes to: when should I do such-and-such? The fact that the questions are always being asked reflects the difficulty of answering them.

Gardening cannot be pre-arranged like the agenda for a meeting. Operations are not dated by the calendar, even though we try to divide the year into four seasons. Seasons vary from year to year, and they vary also from district to district. When I first came to know that the year comprised four seasons, I pictured it as beginning with spring, but I soon realized that spring did not start the year and that winter did not end it.

It was the study of gardening that made me realize how important, and yet elusive, the seasons are. Let us forget the upsets caused when spring is early or late or too wet or too dry. We soon learn that spring comes earlier to some parts of the country than to others. We are then tempted to imagine (wrongly) that we can draw lines of latitude to show spring arriving first in the south and then creeping gradually northwards.

The chief factors which influence the onset of spring are nearness to the sea, height above sea level, and degree of shelter from prevailing winds. Without delving into scientific explanations, it is a fact that the gardening micro-climate may be warmer in some northerly areas than in some southerly ones and may vary between one end of a village and the other.

Let us stay with the question 'When does spring begin?' because the rest of the seasonal problems regarding climate are related to it. We reckon that spring has reached the garden when the mean daily temperature gets above 42°F or 6°C. That temperature has to be exceeded before our native plants can make substantial growth.

Growth will be influenced by other things such as soil fertility, soil moisture and light intensity, but the temperature factor is the vital one we use to indicate the arrival of the gardening spring.

Every fifty feet up from sea level will delay the attainment of that mean temperature by a day and therefore set back spring's arrival by a day. Any normal lateness in the arrival of spring to any specific area is matched by an equal spell of subnormal conditions at the end of the season. That is, a day lost at the beginning of the growing season means another day lost at the end. Since spring will be ten days later in reaching a garden 500 feet up than one at sea level, so the end of summer will be ten days early and the growing season up there will therefore be approximately three weeks shorter than at sea level.

To take an extreme example, in an average season in the British Isles spring will reach Cornwall by mid-February and will not reach the foothills of the Pennines till about five or six weeks later; but the Welsh coast will be in the same bracket as Devon. Add to this the fact that we rarely have an 'average' season and it highlights the difficulty of trying to fix calendar dates for garden operations.

The problems which beset us towards the end of spring are as irritating as those at the beginning. Late spring is the period when night frosts still threaten despite the nearness of summer. These are called radiation frosts, spring frosts or May frosts, and usually come after a very warm, calm, sunny day with a perfectly clear sky.

The hot air rising into the cloudless sky goes steadily up into the very cold layers and, by a movement known as convection, pushes the coldest air to the bottom, bringing frosty air at ground level before the night is over. This helps explain why the valleys and low-lying spots suffer most in such frosts. It also explains why gardeners welcome broken cloud or breezy weather which prevents radiation frosts at this critical season.

Plants which are at risk from spring frosts include summer bedding plants, and such tender food crops as tomatoes and runner beans. Tender subjects need night protection until after the last risk date, which may be some time in May or perhaps early June. This brings us to questions like 'When is it safe to plant outdoor tomatoes?'

There you have a clue how to get the best out of this book. To use this or any other gardening information, you must consider your own garden's micro-climate, particularly such data as the *normal* date of the last spring frost. The emphasis on the word normal is to remind you that we must always be prepared for the abnormal and make allowances. Many experienced gardeners keep five-year diaries in which annual variations are noted. Such notes enable them to estimate the likely dates of the last spring frosts. The less experienced can get helpful advice from local worthies, both amateur and professional, including park-keepers. This sort of local knowledge will help you adapt the timings in the following pages.

It is convenient to divide the year into compartments, and monthly compartments are probably the best. We therefore set out month by month the chief garden operations we might consider doing in the conditions the month might be expected to bring, in an area which fits the norm. If your garden is in an area which is cooler than or later than the norm, you will be behind the calendar of operations at times, because you will make adjustments to suit the general micro-climate of your area.

Later, with experience and skill, you will learn to assess the micro-climate of your own garden. Fences, hedges, buildings and neighbouring high ground may protect you from the coldest winds or, on the contrary, may deprive you of sunshine. Your ground may be light or heavy, sand or clay, free-draining or slow-draining. All these factors will influence your timings.

Whatever operations are allocated to a specific month, there are years when some areas start earlier and there are other years when plenty of areas are behind schedule because of weather fluctuations.

To simplify matters for the reader, the sort of variations most likely to occur have been taken into account by listing reminders in two successive months where operations are extremely sensitive to weather. Thus, if you are baulked one month you will be reminded to catch up in the next month. There are other instances where jobs are listed in successive months for a different reason – because they are repeat jobs which want doing in both months. Such repeats (they apply particularly to what are termed 'successional sowings') are clearly indicated, so that you need neither duplicate a 'one-off' task nor miss out on a useful repetition.

Remember that all the timings given are guidelines. Adapt them to suit your own area and the unpredictable variations in the weather. Always wait till weather and soil are both reasonably near what the job demands. And when in doubt, keep waiting.

CHAPTER TWO

Sowing the Seed

Plants can be propagated by several methods including seed, cuttings, layers and division. One of the wonders of nature is that the little, often minute, seed grains will, under ordinary good growing conditions, develop into plants of considerable size and, according to species, produce an abundance of blooms or an edible crop.

It is advisable to use fresh seed since this is likely to be fully viable, whereas older seed may germinate irregularly. Seed obtained from a reputable source can be depended upon and be in accordance with the Seeds Act requirements. Apart from the loss of money involved, it is a waste of time and effort to buy inferior stock.

In the open ground never sow seed when the soil is cold or wet. Choose a time when the weather looks like remaining mild, remembering there is a proper time for sowing individual subjects as indicated in the monthly work programme, although this is liable to vary according to district and climate.

The smaller the seed the finer should be the soil in

which it is sown. The soil itself should be dry enough to crumble slightly when worked with the hand and both in the open ground and under glass it must never hold together like a pasty mass.

Ideally, the outdoor site should be in a position sheltered from north and east, and in summer sowings do best in partial shade. Break up the soil finely so that air penetrates freely, for seed will not grow under clods. A rich soil is not needed, otherwise growth becomes straggly rather than short and stocky.

Make the bed firm, leaving it a few days before sowing. Draw drills in moist soil, running north to south if possible. Alternatively, seed can be broadcast although this often leads to thick sowing resulting in sickly, drawn specimens.

Depth of sowing depends on the size of the seed. Minute seeds need hardly any covering; in fact, a very light sprinkling of silver sand is usually sufficient. Larger seeds, those that are very slow in germinating, such as phlox, can have up to 13 mm ($\frac{1}{2}$ inch) or more soil over them. Many vegetable seeds including onions and parsnips germinate more readily if the soil is well firmed over them, although this is not necessary in the case of finer seeds. Watering may be required during prolonged dry spells or where greenhouse temperatures are high and the atmosphere dry, but continued overhead watering encourages roots to grow near the surface. It is worth remembering that soil aeration, warmth and moisture are the main requirements for good germination.

THINNING SEEDLINGS

Early thinning of the seedlings is advisable, since small specimens recover from the move quickly with little or no root damage. They should be handled gently and only by the leaves to avoid bruising the stems. Transplant immediately, preferably using a blunt pencil or small trowel to make the holes large enough to prevent the cramping or doubling up of the roots, taking care an air pocket is not left below the roots. Distances of transplanting will depend on the subject.

In the case of carrots, beetroot and onions, the thinning can be done in stages and the later thinnings can be used in the kitchen. In such instances always make certain the soil is firmly pressed back around the seedlings left in the beds or rows. Particularly in warm weather, thinning out should be done in the evening which is the best time to water seedlings if this becomes really necessary during prolonged dry weather. Some annuals and perennials quickly form a few deep, penetrating roots which keep the plants growing well without watering.

PELLETED SEEDS

These are now being used increasingly. Easy to handle, they enable the gardener to space the seeds at precise distances both in the open ground and the greenhouse. Thinning out and the transplanting of seedlings is thus eliminated. The hard inert coating surrounding each seed softens and expands on contact with moisture. Pellets should not be sown deeply or used in very wet soils or the pelleting materials and the seed will become a decaying mass. On the other hand, if the pellets remain in dry soil, the germinating process will not begin, although the soil must not be soaked after sowing or the coating will break down too quickly.

Germination usually takes a couple of days longer than allowed for normal seed.

SOWING UNDER GLASS

Many greenhouse and semi-hardy plants can be raised readily under glass using well drained pots, pans or seed trays of fine moist, porous compost, which should be stored in the greenhouse some days before sowing. Cold compost hinders germination and may spoil the seeds. The John Innes seed compost is very suitable as are the Arthur Bowers and Levington composts. These should be pressed down gently, making a level surface just below the rim of the pots or boxes. Sow thinly, depth again depending on the size of the seeds.

A steady temperature of 15–18°C (60–65°F) is suitable and a sheet of glass and paper should be placed over the pots and boxes lifting them each day to wipe off condensation. Alternatively, the containers can be covered with polythene. Once the seeds have germinated the coverings must be removed and the little plants kept near the glass so that they do not become weak and drawn. Water with care to avoid damping off. A pencil can be used as a dibber when transplanting small seedlings.

Many seeds can be sown in a frame or propagating box, while cloches can be used to cover early vegetable sowings. In all cases good ventilation and careful watering are needed. Early pricking off and planting out are needed to avoid overcrowding and root damage. Half-hardy annuals used for summer bedding, biennials and perennials raised under glass will, of course, need to be gradually hardened off before being moved to their flowering positions.

CHAPTER THREE

January

There is much more to do in January than the casual gardener realizes. Even some enthusiastic gardeners, who do not bestir themselves until spring brings its surge of new life, are surprised when reminded of how much they can be doing so early in the year.

Of course, there are some things which need no reminders. Every keen gardener will busy himself without telling, when dead stems and leaves, old stakes, and all the clutter of the busy season offends the eye in winter. But bleak weather does not stimulate outdoor activity and we tend to put off routine outdoor chores. The temptation should be avoided and these little chores should be tackled during the odd spell of calm weather.

However, there are interesting and useful things that can be done in comfortable surroundings. The seed order, for instance, should not be delayed beyond this month. Catalogues these days are more than mere seed lists. Reading through them and choosing seeds makes pleasant work.

Venture as far as the garden shed or wherever you keep your garden tools and machines. The lawn mower may need a check-up. If you take it to workshops this month you should get it back before the first flush of new growth in the lawn. If you wait till mowing becomes an urgent job, and then discover the need for repair or major maintenance, you may have to wait weeks for servicing. If you do get caught out, find out whether your mower people can hire you a machine while they have yours in for repair. Check up too on cutting tools that need sharpening and oiling.

All this is before you look at the gardening reminders for the month on the following pages. When you look through the reminders you may be tempted to ask whether any of them can be left till February and perhaps better weather. Of course many of them can; the gardening calendar is never inflexible. But putting off means adding to next month's list.

There is a reminder here to prune roses, though you will know that March is the most popular month for it and that there is controversy concerning other months in which it can be done. Without entering into the controversy it can be pointed out that if you want to prune while the bushes are still dormant, this month offers the last chance to do it, because you will find them breaking into growth by next month.

In the general reminders for the vegetable garden, mention is made of liming, and the timing of it. Keep liming and manuring at least six weeks apart. Apply lime to a third of the vegetable plot each year – the part intended for that year's greenstuff.

Fertilizers scattered around the root area of trees, take time to wash in and carry to the roots, so delay there may mean that trees will not be fully nourished at the start of their new growth.

One consolation is that you are not likely to be growing everything to which these comprehensive lists of reminders apply. You may have no fruit trees, or no greenhouse, or only a small patch for vegetables. Study the reminders in the indoor warmth of a winter evening and make a note of things that apply to your garden – a reminder of the reminders, so to speak.

Reminders concerning sowings and plantings apply only when soil and weather permit. In the greenhouse, there are sowings you can make this month but they require a little heat, and the wise gardener will have a heated propagator. You may be puzzled at finding potatoes listed among possible greenhouse plantings. The potatoes are normally planted in pots. Use 23 cm (9 inch) pots, and plant three small potatoes of an early variety in each pot. The crop is ready by the time the pots are wanted for tomato planting. Rhubarb is listed for both indoor and outdoor planting. Indoors it means putting roots in boxes under the staging and hanging some drapes to keep the light out and produce some forced 'sticks'. Outdoor planting can be a routine new planting; digging and dividing old roots; or replanting roots which were dug up in autumn and left exposed to frost – a treatment which helps to stimulate growth when the roots are replanted.

FRUIT

Plant or transplant
Indoors: Vines, peaches and nectarines.
Outdoors: Trees and bushes of all fruits whenever soil and weather permit.

Prune
Indoors: Established grape vines before shoot-buds swell.
Outdoors: Apples, pears, all newly-planted blackberries, raspberries, loganberries, gooseberries; also both new and established bushes of gooseberry, red and white currants.

Spray
Outdoors: All fruit trees and bushes with tar-oil wash to kill over-wintering pest eggs.

Miscellaneous
All prunings should be cleared up and burned promptly to reduce risk of spreading pest and disease troubles. A high-potash general fertilizer can then be scattered around the root area of each tree or bush so that it has time to wash in before emerging

growth demands it. Check fruit ties. Prune newly planted bushes and trained trees. Inspect fruit in store.

VEGETABLES

Sow
Indoors: French beans, cress, carrots, cauliflowers, leeks, lettuce, mustard, onions, radishes, tomatoes.
Outdoors: Under cloches. Broad beans, carrots, onions, peas, spinach.

Plant or transplant
Indoors: Potatoes; bring in rhubarb, chives and mint for forcing; lettuce in greenhouse border.
Outdoors: Rhubarb, lettuce in frames.

Miscellaneous
Indoors: Plan the year's cropping of the vegetable garden. Examine stored cabbages. Start seed potatoes sprouting.
Outdoors: When weather and soil permit, preparation of ground should be treated as an urgent routine job. Fork in bulky ma-

nures or garden compost during digging. Where brassica crops are to be grown, complete such manuring in time to allow about two months before sowing or planting. This will allow lime to be applied during the final soil preparation, bearing in mind that lime and manures must be separated by at least six weeks.

Bend outer leaves over the curds of winter cauliflowers to keep the light off them. Mulch asparagus beds with garden compost.

FLOWERS

Sow
Indoors: Begonia semperflorens, camellia, carnation, gloxinia, lily, pelargonium, petunia, salvia, streptocarpus, sweet pea, verbena.

Plant or transplant
Indoors: Achimenes, tuberous begonia, clivia, gloxinia corms, hippeastrum, hyacinth and bulbous irises. Pot lilies, including *Lilium auratum*, *L. harrisii* and

21

L. speciosum; allow room for top-dressing.
Outdoors: Trees, shrubs, roses.

Prune
Indoors: Cut back stems of Lorraine begonias after flowering.
Outdoors: Roses.

Spray
Indoors: Chrysanthemums and carnations using malathion.

Miscellaneous

Check frequently bowls of bulbs plunged outdoors in frames or sheltered borders. As soon as an inch of growth has been made the bulbs should be brought into cool, light conditions.

Examine dormant bulbous subjects in store for signs of rotting, shrivelling, or mildew. Rotting items should be discarded. Mildew should be dusted with sulphur or Bordeaux powder. If dahlia tubers have shrunk, they can be soaked for a few hours in tepid water to plump them up again. They should then be dried, dusted with sulphur against mildew, and put back into store. Water carefully this month and any necessary damping down should be done early in the day. Dormant achimenes, caladium, canna, gesneria and hippeastrum plants should be kept in a warm, dry place. Do not leave house plants standing in saucers of water.

CHAPTER FOUR

February

We can expect noticeable signs of returning spring and begin serious planning this month for both the decorative and edible parts of the garden. February can be a stormy month and it is wise to examine newly planted roses, trees and shrubs, re-firming the soil around the roots and checking supports and ties.

Many hard wooded deciduous (not evergreen) trees and shrubs can be pruned when there is an absence of frost. Learn to prune with a purpose, studying individual growth habit, the way flowers and fruit are borne, and the season. Generally speaking the more vigorous growing subjects require less pruning, since cutting stimulates even stronger growth.

Where there is room, this is a good time to make a rock garden. Select an open, sunny, well-drained position. Half bury the stones and fill the spaces between them with good soil, making little pockets for individual plants. Avoid placing large stones at the highest part of the garden.

Press on with the digging of vacant ground whenever the soil is neither wet nor frost bound. Any alterations being planned for beds and borders can be carried out this month, attention being paid to paths that need making up.

In the greenhouse, the top ventilators should be opened during the middle of the day so long as draughts are avoided and there are no severe frosts. As the days lengthen, gradually increase watering but be guided by the indoor temperature and the plants you are growing.

Autumn sown peas can be helped to grow well by drawing up the soil towards the plants with an occasional dusting of lime. Stock of many hardy shrubs can be increased by pegging down lower branches into the soil.

Frost and other winter weather often loosens the soil around rock garden plants. Re-firm the soil and as necessary renew labels. Scatter slug pellets among the plants since pests are often active during mild weather.

If fruit trees, hedging and shrubs on order arrive during severe weather they should be kept in a frost-free shed with roots protected until conditions improve.

FRUIT

Sow
Indoors: Melons, towards end of month.

Plant or transplant
Indoors: Apricots, figs, nectarines, peaches and vines. Bring in pot-grown strawberries for forcing.
Outdoors: As January. Strawberries. Grape vines from pots, selecting a sunny, sheltered position.

Prune
Outdoors: Cut down newly planted black currants to encourage basal growths. Shorten laterals on cordon apples to 3 or 4 buds and remove old wood from acid cherries.

Spray
Indoors: Vine rods, during mild weather. Lightly syringe peach and nectarine flowers with water to assist fruit setting.
Outdoors: Apples, pears, plums, blackberries, loganberries, raspberries. Spray black currants against big-bud at the late

25

grape stage, and gooseberries against mildew.

Miscellaneous
All plants should be examined frequently for signs of diseases or pests and the necessary steps taken to control these disorders. Regular ventilation without draughts is a help in this direction. Hand pollinating nectarines and peaches is an aid in securing a good crop. Untie and retrain canes of blackberries and loganberries to make fruit gathering easier. All cane fruits will benefit from an application of potash around the root area. Early-flowering wall-trained fruit trees should be given some light night protection if possible when frosts are forecast.

VEGETABLES

Sow
Indoors: Aubergine, dwarf beans, broccoli, Brussels sprouts, cress, capsicum, celery, celeriac, cauliflowers, cucumbers, herbs, mustard, lettuce, radishes, tomatoes. Broad

beans for planting out. Mung beans and other 'sprouters'.

Outdoors: Broccoli, Brussels sprouts, broad beans, early carrots, cabbages, cauliflowers, lettuce, leeks, marrows, onions, peas, parsnips, parsley, radishes, summer spinach, spinach beet, turnips.

Plant or transplant

Indoors: Early cucumbers, tomatoes.

Outdoors: Jerusalem artichokes, globe artichoke suckers, asparagus, over-wintered Brussels sprouts, box-raised celery, herbs, horseradish, onions, potatoes, rhubarb, seakale and shallots.

Prune

Indoors: Pinch out cucumber laterals to prevent overcrowding, straggling growth and to ensure even distribution of fruit. Once melons reach top of their supports, pinch out growing points to encourage laterals. Remove side-shoots from tomatoes.

Spray

Indoors: Melons before shutting ventilators in the evening but reduce overhead syringings as the plants come into flower.

Miscellaneous

Many plants in frames can be hardened off. Avoid doing this too quickly or growth will be checked, or too slowly, which causes thin, drawn growth. Apart from crops sown in pots or boxes for planting in the open later, and this includes runner beans, cauliflowers and sweet corn, others can be sown for maturing *in situ*, including beetroot, carrots, lettuce, radishes and turnips. When making a new seed bed, any sifted bonfire ashes or old soot raked into the surface will be of great benefit. Established asparagus beds can be dressed with decayed manure or rich compost.

FLOWERS

Sow

Indoors: Abutilon, floss flower (ageratum), pimpernel (anagallis), snapdragon (antirrhinum), begonia, canna, cockscomb (celosia), cups and saucers (cobaea), carnation, cascade chrysanthemums, dahlia, pink (dianthus), gloxinia, busy lizzy (impatiens), burning bush (kochia), lobelia, marigold, nemesia, tobacco plant (nicotiana), petunia, cape primrose (streptocarpus), sage (salvia), salpiglossis, butterfly flower (schizanthus), sea lavender (statice), sweet pea, vervain (verbena) and ten-week stock.

Plant or transplant

Indoors: Carnation, chrysanthemum. Start achimenes tubers, begonia, and dahlia. Pot on tomato seedlings. Divide and re-pot canna, fuchsia.

Outdoors: Deciduous trees, shrubs, roses, lilies (except *Lilium candidum*), anemones, buttercup (ranunculus) hardy herbaceous perennials. Lift and divide Christmas rose.

Prune

Indoors: Bougainvillea, fuchsia, zonal and ivy-leaved pelargonium.

Outdoors: Caryopteris clandonensis, clematis (jackmanii group, and other late-summer flowerers), hydrangea *Spiraea* x *bumalda*, *Spiraea japonica*, and *Tamarisk pentandra*.

Miscellaneous

As woody plants spring into new life, watch for evidence of dying back. Cut out dead wood and any that looks diseased. Check your daffodils for leaves with yellow streaks in them, because this symptom often indicates a virus disease and infected plants should go on the bonfire.

In mild, sheltered areas, where lawns started into early growth, a light mowing can be made when the grass is free from frost and fairly dry. Set the mower blades fairly high for the first cut.

Cover the ground with cloches towards the end of the month to warm the soil, thus helping to promote germination for the early outdoor sowings.

CHAPTER FIVE

March

We now say 'farewell to winter, welcome spring'. Soon there will be very noticeable changes in plant growth; roots will become active, buds will break and very early flowers will appear.

Following winter rains the soil often becomes hard packed, although this is less likely if humus-forming material has been regularly worked into the ground. Decayed manure is most valuable, since, apart from the nitrogen it supplies, there is the beneficial physical effect provided by the organic matter.

Assuming that the soil has been properly prepared, there remains a subject particularly important in the vegetable garden – rotation. The same piece of ground used continuously for similar crops becomes exhausted of essential feeding matter, with the greater possibility of weaker growth being attacked by pests and diseases.

A simple four-year rotation would be (1) brassicas (2) rootcrops (3) peas and beans (4) miscellaneous vegetables. These will ensure the ground is left in good condition for the following year's crop.

In the flower garden, the older clumps of perennial plants can be divided. Break them into smallish pieces, discard the hard central portions, and plant only the young outer pieces. Replant with a trowel, working fine soil around the roots. There is still time to move wall-flowers, forget-me-nots, Canterbury bells and double daisies which could not be planted out in autumn.

On previously well prepared sites, turves can be laid. Place them close together, work in fine soil and beat them down before rolling.

In the greenhouse, make sure the glass is kept clean so that all possible light is admitted. This also applies to frames and cloches. A steady temperature around 15°C (60°F) and good ventilation should ensure healthy growth. The lengthening days will cause carnations to grow faster. They will need tying, disbudding and feeding. Cacti and succulents will need more water as growth develops. House plants, too, will need more moisture. Remove weak or diseased shoots and apply liquid manure sparingly.

FRUIT

Plant or transplant

Indoors: Pot-grown apples, pears, gages and cherries can now be brought from outdoors into the cool greenhouse.

Outdoors: Apples, apricots, blackberries, cherries, currants, figs, gooseberries, grape vines, loganberries, mulberries, nectarines, nuts, peaches, pears, plums, raspberries.

Prune

Indoors: Trained trees removing weak, badly placed shoots and carefully tying in young vine laterals.

Outdoors: Late planted apples, pears, damsons, cob and filbert nuts, autumn fruiting raspberries, quinces. Cut down newly planted blackberries and loganberries to within 18–25 cm (9–10 inches) of ground level. Shorten stems of recently planted gooseberries and red currants by one half and raspberries to within 15 cm (6 inches) from the base. Tops of established canes can be shortened to a strong bud.

Spray

Indoors: All young growths at first sight of greenfly.

Outdoors: Peaches and nectarines (with lime-sulphur) against leaf curl. Dormant fruit trees with tar-oil winter wash. Renew grease bands where necessary.

Miscellaneous

Tread down the soil around all recently planted trees, bushes and strawberry plants for frosts often loosen the ground. If cloches are available, some can be used to cover strawberry plants for earlier fruiting. This is a good time to examine black currant bushes for signs of big-bud.

Soft fruit bushes will benefit if mulched with decayed manure or compost when the ground is fairly dry, while wood ashes or potash fertilizer will strengthen black currant and gooseberry bushes. Complete soil preparation for new fruit trees and bushes being planted shortly.

Indoors, peaches, nectarines and apricots should be hand-pollinated.

VEGETABLES

Sow

Indoors: Aubergines, French beans, Brussels sprouts, shorthorn carrots, cauliflowers, celery, cress, leeks, lettuce, mustard, onions, radishes, tomatoes.

Outdoors: In sheltered places or under cloches sow broad beans, corn salad, onions, parsnips, parsley, early peas, turnips, round-seeded spinach. Beetroot under cloches.

Plant or transplant

Indoors: Plant and force seakale in pots or boxes. Pot on autumn sown lettuce seedlings.

Outdoors: Jerusalem artichokes, spring cabbage, garlic, onion sets, autumn sown onions, early potatoes in warm sheltered places, shallots. Divide and replant rhubarb.

Spray

Any overwintering vegetables indoors or outdoors suffering from mildew, using benomyl or a similar wash.

Miscellaneous

Excepting during very frosty weather, frames and cloches covering cauliflowers, Brussel sprouts, lettuce, etc, should be kept well ventilated.

Any vacancies in the herb border should be made good and the whole surface dressed with well-sifted leaf mould or compost.

Prepare trenches for celery, leeks and runner beans but do not leave them 'open'.

Slugs are now likely to be *more* prevalent, moving about in damp, mild weather which is the best time to put down slug bait. Make small heaps; cover them with a slate or tile for protection from rain and to prevent animals or birds eating it.

FLOWERS

Sow

Indoors: As February. Annuals for pot culture, aster, auricula, *Chrysanthemum indicum* 'Charm', coleus, kalanchoë, *Primula obconica*, *Primula sinensis*, solanum, summer bedding plants, herbaceous perennials, zinnia.

Outdoors: Hardy annuals including alyssum, bartonia, calendula, candytuft, clarkia, annual coreopsis, cornflower, eschscholzia, godetia, gypsophila, larkspur, lavatera, linum, malope, nemophila, nigella, phacelia, poppies, Virginian stock and the annual forms of saponaria, rudbeckia.

Plant or transplant

Indoors: Pot on over-wintered annuals, asparagus fern, begonia, coleus, croton, calceolaria, canna, fuchsia, gloxinia, pelargonium, smithiantha. Pot up rooted chrysanthemums, and cuttings of dahlia, fuchsia, cyclamen seedlings and bedding plants. Re-pot palms, smilax, aspidistra, house plants.

Outdoors: Alpines, hardy climbers, border carnations, gladiolus, montbretia, herbaceous perennials, polyanthus, roses, sweet peas, deciduous trees and shrubs, anemone tubers.

Prune

Indoors: Bouvardia and any climbing plants. Cut back poinsettia stems by a half. Remove faded flower stems from hippeastrums.

Outdoors: Buddleia davidii, hardy fuchsias, bush, standard and climbing roses. Any shrubs or plants damaged by frosts.

Spray

Indoors: Carnations, pinks. Syringe *Azalea indica* to encourage new growth.

Outdoors: Any plants affected by mildew or rust.

Miscellaneous

Indoors: Take cuttings of Rex and winter flowering begonias, *Campanula isophylla*, dahlia, heliotrope and marguerite. Calceolarias as well as potted annuals will benefit if given light supports while young fuchsia and geranium plants and sweet peas sown in January should have their growing point removed. Many orchids can now be re-potted, and the plants should be shaded from strong sunlight. When the soil is easily workable, prepare the sites for new lawns and for the repair to old ones.

CHAPTER SIX

April

This is the month of sunshine and showers, when growth usually makes rapid progress. Weeds now flower quickly, their self-sown seeds producing numerous offspring which should be destroyed while small. In some seasons, strong spring winds loosen or may blow down climbing plants and wall subjects, including trained fruit trees. It is therefore advisable to check trees and climbers so that branches and stems can be re-fastened as necessary. Sometimes, too, it is necessary to protect the blossoms of fruit trees on walls while a syringing of liquid derris will kill off greenfly.

If late frosts touch plants that have not been fully hardened off, make sure they are shaded before the sun reaches them and spray with *cold* water which allows gradual thawing out. Late frosts may also damage early potato foliage. As the first leaves appear, draw the soil over them to form protective ridges. Should frosts still threaten, give the leaves a night covering of straw.

Once cloches and frames have been cleared of crops

the soil can be raked well, a good sprinkling of compost worked in and further sowings of lettuce, other salad crops or sweet corn can be made.

Preparations for summer bedding must now be made and daffodils and other early bulbs that have finished flowering can be lifted and replanted in an odd corner or spare ground, so the foliage dies down naturally. This will make it possible to prepare the ground for bedding plants. Feed shrub and herbaceous borders with Growmore at 70 g a sq m (2 oz a sq yd).

This, too, is the time to think of outdoor window boxes, hanging baskets and tubs with a view to a summer and autumn display. Choose plants that will stand up to the wind. Shade-loving subjects will be most successful in north-facing positions.

In the greenhouse, some subjects that have been flowering throughout the winter should now be encouraged to rest, including freesias and cyclamen.

Indoor cucumbers need attention now. Pinch out the tips of side-shoots as soon as they have grown to 20–22 cm (8–9 inches). Secondary side-shoots need pinching once two leaves have formed.

Lawns will require more frequent cutting, but do not do it when the surface is wet or frozen.

FRUIT

Sow
Indoors: Melon

Plant or transplant
Indoors: Late vines for pots.
Outdoors: Raspberries, strawberry runners.

Prune
Indoors: Continue to train melons, restricting each plant to about four fruits, spaced evenly over the 'vines'. Hand-pollinate the female flowers. By judicious pinching-out it is possible to produce a batch of flowers which open all at the same time. The earliest peaches will be setting fruit and a little thinning is advisable.
Outdoors: Currants, red and white, left unpruned in winter; young trained plums. Cut back freshly planted raspberry canes. Remove badly-placed shoots from trained trees and pull out all suckers.

Spray

Indoors: Pot-grown and trained trees. Fine mist sprays of water about midday when flowers are opening provide a fruit-setting atmosphere.

Outdoors: Apples and pears with benomyl, carbendazim or captan to control scab; gooseberries and black currants with benomyl or thiophanate-methyl to control mildew and leaf spot. Regular spraying of black currant bushes with benomyl will suppress the mites that cause big-bud. Alternatively, remove the infected buds as soon as you see them. A fine mist spray of water will help fruit of wall-trained peaches and nectarines to set. Watch for blackfly in tips of cherries and peaches and apply an insecticide.

Miscellaneous

Give free ventilation on sunny days to strawberry plants being forced in greenhouses or frames.

The earliest vines will now be 'stoning' or forming pips and severe fluctuations in temperature must be avoided. Continue to remove badly placed shoots from trained trees. Mulch raspberries, blackberries and loganberries with well-rotted manure, or compost, which will both feed the plants and keep roots moist.

Remove flowers from spring-planted strawberries.

VEGETABLES

Sow

Indoors: French beans, runner beans, celery, courgettes, marrows, tomatoes. To raise plants for cloche work or outdoor planting in late May, sow cucumbers and marrows at the end of the month.

Outdoors: Globe artichokes, asparagus, round beetroot, broad beans, sprouting broccoli, Brussels sprouts, cabbage, cauliflowers, cress, endive, herbs, kale, kohl rabi, lettuce, mustard, salad onions, parsley, peas, radishes, salsify, savoys, spinach beet, turnips.

Plant or transplant

Indoors: Celery, cucumbers, tomatoes.

Outdoors: Artichokes, asparagus, broad beans, cauliflowers, summer cabbage, onions including sets, peas, potatoes, rooted herb cuttings.

Miscellaneous

Celery trenches enriched with plenty of manure should be prepared without delay as should marrow beds, but they do not need to be raised. If slugs are troublesome, slug bait should be put down while dustings of soot also may be applied to the ground. Harden off onions, Brussels sprouts, cauliflowers and the like ready for planting out in the open. Plant asparagus early in the month.

Once the earliest growths of asparagus are 10–15 cm (4–6 inches) above the soil, cut them 25 mm (1 inch) below soil level and take them to eat.

Pull up old stumps of cabbages, Brussels sprouts and any other brassicas. If left, they become breeding places for whitefly and grey root aphids.

Some of the earliest vegetable sowings such as spinach will need thinning. Cover potato foliage if frosts threaten. Remove rhubarb flowers as soon as seen. Place manure or compost around globe artichokes. Order tomato plants if necessary, for outdoor planting in June.

FLOWERS

Sow

Indoors: Cineraria, coleus, exacum, *Primula kewensis, P. obconica, P. sinensis,* zinnia, half-hardy annuals for flowering in pots and other containers.

Outdoors: Half-hardy annuals as March, aster, canary creeper, bedding dahlia, dimorphotheca, layia, leptosiphon, *Dorotheanthus bellidiformis* (syn. *Mesembryanthemum criniflorum*), nasturtiums, nicotiana, salpiglossis, sweet sultan, *Tagetes tenuifolia pumila,* ursinia, venidium, zinnia, biennials, ornamental grasses and lawn grass seed.

Plant or transplant

Indoors: Achimenes, azalea, annuals, begonia, bedding plants, carnation, chrysanthemum, camellia, cyclamen, dahlia, eupatorium, gloxinia, haemanthus, jasminum, luculia, pelargonium, solanum.

Outdoors: Alpines, antirrhinum, gladiolus, herbaceous perennials, montbretia, pansy, penstemon, sweet pea, viola, evergreen shrubs.

Prune

Indoors: As March, azalea, deutzia, genista, early flowering shrubs which have flowered on previous season's growth.

Outdoors: As March, evergreen foliage shrubs, *Buddleia davidii* varieties, forsythia, *Leycesteria formosa, Perovskia atriplicifolia,* romneya, willows grown for coloured bark. Clip ivy and box edging.

Spray

Indoors: Look out for insect pests, particularly aphids, and spray as necessary.

Miscellaneous

Look over the advancing growth of roses and, should leaves be curling, search for caterpillars and other pests causing the trouble. Hand pick or spray to destroy them.

Gardeners who have no greenhouse or other glass covering can start dahlia tubers in boxes of peaty soil or, in well-drained ground, plant them directly into flowering positions. Plant out March sown sweet pea seedlings and take out side shoots and tendrils from the early sown plants now growing strongly.

This is a good time to plant evergreen shrubs and hedging plants. Make sure the soil is moist, plant firmly, and retread the soil from time to time since winds often loosen the roots.

Press on with the planting of gladiolus, placing the corms of the large-flowered varieties at least 10 cm (4 inches) deep, otherwise the heavy spikes will topple.

Before planting out border chrysanthemums, see that the soil is well prepared so the plants have a good start. Give them plenty of room to develop properly and 45–60 cm ($1\frac{1}{2}$–2 ft) should be regarded as the minimum distance apart. Put supports in first, so that roots are not damaged, and tie the plants immediately. Supports should be given to the taller-growing delphiniums, before the stems become misshapen.

CHAPTER SEVEN

May

There should be much colour in the garden now, with attractive displays in beds and borders. Fruit trees and bushes will add their blossoms to the rainbow effect. Weeds increase, so also do the songs of birds. Frost may still occur at night and steps need to be taken to give protection to certain subjects as detailed last month.

Good lawns do much to set off the colourful parts of the garden and if you sowed seed earlier this year, when the grass is 5–7 cm (2–3 inches) high, it can be topped, the mower being set high. A sharp scythe can be used. Avoid cutting too close during the first season. May is a good month to use lawn sand to kill small broad-leaved weeds on established lawns. Apply it in accordance with the maker's instructions.

During spells of dry weather, it may be necessary to water newly planted subjects. Do this in the morning or evening and give good soakings – not sprinklings, which merely bring the roots nearer the surface. Keep up the war against weeds, to prevent self-seeding and save much work during the next few months.

Climbers and creeping wall plants often grow into an unsightly tangle. If they are kept trained and loosely tied in, they will look neat and be a credit to the garden. If neglected for a season, it is difficult to restore them to shapeliness. Roses, too, should be looked over so that badly placed or overcrowded shoots can be removed. Aim to keep the centre of the bushes 'open'.

Water-lilies and other aquatic plants transplant well this month. According to depth of water, some can be planted directly into soil at the bottom of the pool or placed in baskets or pots sunk into position. By the former method, it is best to empty the pool first and then plant, and allow the water to rise gradually.

In the fruit garden, trees and bushes will benefit from a mulch of manure round their roots. Raspberry suckers should be thinned out leaving four to six canes to each stool. Strawy litter placed around strawberries will keep the developing fruit clean. Runners not required for propagation should be cut off.

Proper greenhouse management is important now. As the sun gains power, plants need shading. Foliage plants, particularly, may suffer if exposed to periods of intense light and sunshine. Much more water and increased ventilation are other requirements. Early peaches and nectarines, now ripening their fruits, must no longer be sprayed.

FRUIT

Plant
Outdoors: Container-grown trees and bushes.

Prune

Indoors: Melons; pinch back peach, nectarine and apricot shoots.
Outdoors: Thin raspberry canes. Shorten or rub out new growth on peaches. Keep fan-trained trees shapely. Remove unwanted strawberry runners.

Bark-ring over-vigorous apples and pears.

Spray

Indoors: In hot weather, syringe with water all trained and pot-grown specimens.
Outdoors: Apples, pears, cherries, black currants, gooseberries, peaches, nectarines, strawberries.

Miscellaneous

The roots of trained trees growing against walls and fences will benefit from a good soaking of water while an occasional overhead syringing will help to keep the foliage

49

healthy. Continue to pull out all unwanted raspberry suckers. If you intend to exhibit gooseberries later, some fruit thinning must be done this month.

Young fruit trees should not be allowed to produce too much fruit, and the crop can be limited by rubbing out some of the flower clusters.

A spraying of derris just before the flowers open should control sawfly, which often attacks very early.

Look over bush peaches. To keep them a good shape, cut out badly placed and crowded branches.

Keep weeds away from the base of all fruit trees, bushes and canes.

VEGETABLES

Sow

Indoors: Runner and dwarf beans for planting outdoors next month. Carrots, salad plants, tomatoes, cauliflowers for October use.

Outdoors: Dwarf French and runner beans, beetroot, chicory, cress, ridge cucumbers, endive, herbs, kohl rabi, lettuce, marrows, mustard, peas, radishes, spinach, turnips.

Plant or transplant
Indoors: Celery, cucumbers, tomatoes.
Outdoors: French beans (from boxes), Brussels sprouts, cabbages, cauliflowers, celeriac, chicory, ridge cucumbers, leeks, marrows, onions, parsley, peas, potatoes, pumpkins, sweet corn.

Prune
Indoors: Keep side-shoots removed from tomato plants.

Spray

Indoors: Cucumbers, tomatoes to clear mildew and whitefly.
Outdoors: Treat carrots and onions against 'fly'; turnips and swedes against flea-beetles and other vegetables when attacked by aphids.

Miscellaneous
Seedlings of beetroot, lettuce, onions, parsnips and turnips should be thinned out before they become thin and drawn. When ground has been cleared of green crops the soil should be well dug and manured in readiness for summer lettuce, celery and outdoor tomatoes. Sites should also be prepared for marrows.

Keep peas and runner beans well supported and if the soil between the rows is mulched with rotted manure or compost it will prevent drying out and provide extra feeding matter.

Cuttings of herbs including sage and thyme will now root readily if inserted in a shady spot where the soil remains moist.

FLOWERS

Sow
Indoors: Achimenes, calceolaria, cineraria, coleus, gloxinia, hippeastrum, stocks (giant and Brompton forms).
Outdoors: Hardy annuals, aquilegia, aster, auricula, Canterbury bells, cobaea, delphinium, forget-me-not, foxglove, night-scented stock, oriental poppy, polyanthus, primrose, wallflower.

Plant or transplant
Indoors: Begonia, carnation, chrysanthemum, coleus, fuchsia, ferns, pelargonium, streptocarpus.
Outdoors: Alpines, antirrhinum, aquatics, summer bedding plants (late in the month), border chrysanthemum, dormant dahlia tubers, magnolia, pansy, penste-

mon (from frames), hardy perennial seedlings, viola, violet, zonal pelargonium.

Prune

Indoors: Fuchsias to encourage shapeliness. Pinch back long straggly growths on house plants.

Outdoors: Berberis stenophylla and other early flowering shrubs (not those producing ornamental berries), lilac and rhododendron, simply removing old flower heads. Pinch out centre tips of outdoor chrysanthemums. Cut back *Prunus triloba* and flowering currant when flowering is finished.

Spray

Indoors: Control aphids with a systemic insecticide.

Outdoors: Lilies, against aphids and botrytis. Roses, using a combined insecticide and fungicide for mildew and rust. Apply liquid derris for caterpillars and aphids on perennial and annual plants.

Miscellaneous

Indoors: Top-dress stem-rooting lilies in pots. Continue to support and tie in perpetual flowering carnations. Harden off gradually all plants under glass that are to be planted outdoors. This will allow more room to be given to cineraria, primula and other plants as they are potted on.

Some light shading will be necessary this month, although it is too early to provide permanent blinds for greenhouses or frames.

Hydrangea cuttings can be taken, to produce flowering plants for next year. Select non-flowering shoots about 10 cm (4 inches) long and insert them round the edge of 8 cm ($3\frac{1}{2}$ inch) pots of a rooting compost in a propagator with a temperature of 16°C (60°F).

Feed house plants and keep them from draughts and strong, scorching sun. *Outdoors:* If you have double flowering strains of plants such as arabis, sweet rocket and lychnis which are unlikely to come true from seed, they can be propagated from cuttings taken this month, or side-shoots can be rooted in the same way.

CHAPTER EIGHT

June

Gradual transformation occurs in the garden this month. Most spring flowers go over, while roses and many other summer flowers appear in quick succession.

Watering during spells of dry weather may be needed since plants will now transpire at a greater rate, and moisture will be lost from the soil by evaporation as the warmth of the sun increases. Always apply really good soakings rather than surface sprinklings which encourage surface rooting and make matters worse.

With so many, varied jobs to do outside, it is easy to overlook the greenhouse requirements. Shading and ventilation must be attended to. Pot plants will need occasional feeds of weak liquid manure.

If you require roses for showing or blooms with really long stems, the clusters of flowers can be disbudded, leaving the main bud, by simply nipping out the other buds with the finger and thumb.

Cold winds can play havoc with tender young plants; and even in mild areas exposed country gardens sometimes get spring frosts during the first week.

When planting out tender subjects such as tomatoes or dahlia plants (as distinct from dahlia tubers), be prepared to put on cloches or erect a temporary screen (such as a polythene 'fence') if cold winds threaten before the plants are settled in.

No sooner does summer reach us than it starts to go away, and since the month brings the longest day it must obviously see the days begin to shorten, so that plants get a reduced daily quota of essential light.

If you sow peas now, choose an early variety because such varieties are quicker to mature and time is getting short. This sowing may need spraying against mildew in August or September.

FRUIT

Prune

Indoors: Grape vines, removing superfluous and weak young shoots to prevent overcrowding. Carefully thin the berries. Help peaches, nectarines and apricots to ripen by removing a leaf here and there to expose the fruit to the sun. Peaches and nectarines still need disbudding to encourage formation of next season's fruit spurs.
Outdoors: Commence summer pruning of gooseberries and red and white currants, doing the job gradually over several weeks.

Remove breast wood from wall trees. Prune plums when in full leaf because that is the stage where there is less danger of attack by the silver leaf fungus. Cover wounds with white lead paint or grafting wax.

Spray

Indoors: Whiteflies multiply rapidly, particularly where tomatoes are being grown. Remedies include pyrethrum, malathion or bioresmethrin spray, and biological predators.

Outdoors: All fruit trees, bushes and canes attacked by aphids or caterpillars. Pears, apples and plums against mildew and scab. If plum aphis is suspected spray with malathion. Raspberries and other cane fruit as soon as they begin to colour using derris in liquid or powder form. Spray strawberries against grey mould. Syringe cherries against blackfly.

Miscellaneous

Keep newly grafted shoots on fruit trees securely tied, and the shoots of trained trees fastened into position.

Examine vines growing against walls and see that all weak and superfluous growths are removed. Allow only one bunch of grapes on each spur, removing the weaker cluster.

The new growths of black currants can be encouraged by mulching the soil with rotted manure. Since the bushes root near the surface, avoid deep hoeing by not permitting the growth of perennial weeds.

When they have made six or seven leaves, pinch out the tops of the laterals on fan-trained fruit trees, where not required for extension or replacement.

Peaches and nectarines in the greenhouse should be given free ventilation so long as the weather is mild. The ripening will be assisted by removing a few leaves to expose fruit to full light and sun. Once trees have been cleared of fruit, syringe them several times a day with clean water, to freshen the foliage and prevent the appearance of red spider mite and thrips.

VEGETABLES

Sow

Indoors: Mustard and cress each week rather than in one large batch. Provide moisture and shade.

Outdoors: Successional sowings of dwarf French beans, beetroot, carrots, chicory, endive, lettuce, radishes, dwarf peas, swedes, turnips, salad crops and spinach.

Plant or transplant

Indoors: Another batch of tomato plants if required; late cucumbers. Thin out any seedlings in pots or trays.

Outdoors: Brussels sprouts, celery, celeriac, leeks, marrows, purple sprouting broccoli, Savoy cabbages, tomatoes, winter cabbages. Vegetable marrows and pumpkins from frames. Plant leeks by making holes with a dibber and dropping the plants in. Do not firm them but water the plants so that soil is washed over the roots.

Prune

Indoors: Stop cucumber laterals and renovate plants by removing old laterals and training young shoots in their place. Pinch out side-shoots of melons.

Outdoors: Keep side-shoots removed from tomatoes.

Spray

Indoors: Aubergines, cucumbers, melons, tomatoes, peppers against grey mould, mildew and botrytis.

Outdoors: All vegetables, at first sightings of any aphids and caterpillars. If vegetable garden is surrounded by hedges, these too, should be sprayed, since they often harbour pests and disease. Also, clear weeds from hedge bases which harbour blackfly.

Feed: In greenhouse, aubergines, cucumbers, peppers, tomatoes.

Miscellaneous

During hot weather, greenhouse, frame and cloche glass should be lightly shaded. This will prevent cucumbers, tomatoes and other covered crops being scorched.

Continue to regulate the growths of cucumbers, and, if white roots appear through the surface soil, apply a top dressing of rich soil.

Potatoes should be earthed up when the soil is just moist. In light soil, leave ridges rather wide at the top to catch rain. Tread down the soil around Brussels sprouts and winter cabbages so that firm heads develop.

Weeding and hoeing are routine tasks this month. Many pests become active. Derris is a safe insecticide against aphids, caterpillars, etc., on food crops.

A sprinkling of nitro-chalk around seakale plants will lead to much stronger growth.

The cutting of asparagus should cease before the end of the month so that plants can produce a good crop next year. Refill all spaces from which crops have been harvested.

FLOWERS

Sow

Indoors: Anemone coronaria 'St Brigid', calceolaria, dwarf campanulas, linaria, saxifrages and hardy primulas *Primula malacoides, P. sinensis* and *P. obconica*.

Outdoors: Annuals to provide autumn flowering plants, biennials and perennials treated as biennials to flower next year, including Brompton stock, Canterbury bell (*Campanula medium*), honesty (*Lunaria annua*), iceland poppy (*Papaver nudicaule*), sweet william (*Dianthus barbatus*), Siberian wallflower (*Cheiranthus allionii*), pansy (*Viola tricolor*) and polyanthus (*Primula* x *media*). Hardy perennials include anchusa, aubrieta, catmint (*Nepeta mussinii*), delphinium, lupin, midsummer daisy or fleabane (erigeron), pinks (*Dianthus plumaris*), pyrethrum, sea holly (eryngium) and Tibetan poppy (*Meconopsis betonicifolia*).

Plant or transplant

Indoors: Cuttings of *Begonia rex* and saintpaulias in pots or trays of peaty compost. Make up hanging baskets and indoor bowls and boxes. Move carnation cuttings to 13–15 cm (5 or 6 inch) pots.

Outdoors: Last of the bedding plants – half-hardy annuals sown under glass in March and April including ageratum, alyssum, snapdragon (antirrhinum), dahlia, dimorphotheca, dorotheanus (mesembryanthemum), morning glory (ipomoea), kingfisher daisy (felicia), *Gomphrena globosa* (globe amaranth), marigolds (French and African), monkey flower (mimulus), bells of Ireland (molucella), nemesia, tobacco plant (nicotiana), petunia, *Phlox drummondii*, portulaca, salpiglossis, salvia, butterfly flower (schizanthus), tagetes, ornamental maize, ursinia, verbena, zinnia.

Divide and replant hardy primulas and flag irises. Rhizomes of the latter should be placed just level with the surface soil. Cut off the top half of the leaves.

Pot on in the greenhouse young cyclamen, coleus, carnation, late chrysanthemum, cape primrose (streptocarpus), winter-flowering begonia, hydrangea cuttings.

Prune

Indoors: Rose 'Maréchal Niel' and similar climbing roses that have finished flowering in the greenhouse; also other ornamental climbers, such as *Genista fragrans*. Cut back regal pelargoniums.

Outdoors: Early flowering shrubs including *Diervilla florida* (*Weigela florida*), deutzia, escallonia, mock orange (philadelphus), chaenomeles ('japonica'). Pinch out sideshoots on cordon-grown sweet peas. Cut back aubrieta and other rampant-growing spring flowering rock-plants. Disbud carnations.

Spray

Indoors: Give frequent sprayings of liquid derris or other insecticide to all plants, to keep them free from greenfly. Use a fungicide if botrytis or mildew is seen. Frequent syringings of water will keep down red spider mite. Water and feed in greenhouse all pot plants which are in full growth. This also applies to house plants. If you go away for a few days or more, make sure provision is made for their care including watering, feeding and shade from direct sunshine.

Outdoors: Spray sweet peas, roses and chrysanthemums to control greenfly and caterpillars. Spray roses against black spot and spray or dust wallflowers and similar seedlings with derris to destroy flea beetles.

Miscellaneous

Tall-growing herbaceous plants and lilies need to be kept firmly staked to prevent wind damage and possible breakage. Sweet peas also need attention. To ensure that they continue to produce large florets, the roots must not become dry. After soaking the soil, apply a mulch of strawy manure, failing which leaf mould or peat can be used with feeds of liquid manure at ten-day intervals. Rose stocks can be budded from the middle of the month but not during very dry weather. Buds should be chosen from firm young stock. On the same subject, if you grafted any fruit trees last spring, they should now be examined to make sure the raffia or other ties used are not strangling the scion. Early flowering and decorative chrysanthemums need stopping according to whether many small or a few large blooms are required.

If you are growing large-flowered violets make sure you remove the runners which form so readily at this time of year. The first and strongest runner can be grown on if required for propagation. Otherwise, nip them all out or the plants will become weakened and the flowers very small.

Plants of the winter cherry (*Solanum capsicastrum*) raised from seed or cuttings can be placed in the cold frame or other sheltered position outdoors. There they should flower and berry well if given occasional overhead syringings of water. Take the plants indoors in autumn when the berries begin to colour.

CHAPTER NINE

July

The garden should present a pleasing appearance, with flower and vegetable crops developing well and the fruit harvest beginning.

This means there will be more time to potter in the garden, doing those little, but often important jobs, that may have had to be put off during past weeks. Weeding, lawn mowing, taking off dead flowers and building up the compost heap will all occupy time while various plants may require staking. Layering of border carnations and various shrubs can be done this month.

The discovery of pests or other plant troubles will need immediate action.

Earwigs are often troublesome at this time. Attacked plants should be cleared of weeds and sprayed with an insecticide such as carbaryl or trichlorphon to stop the pests climbing.

Lawns will benefit from being aerated. There is a special tool for this purpose, or a garden fork can be used. Fusarium and similar lawn disorders can be controlled by a fungicide.

High humidity and frequent rains encourage these diseases but early spraying and dusting will control them.

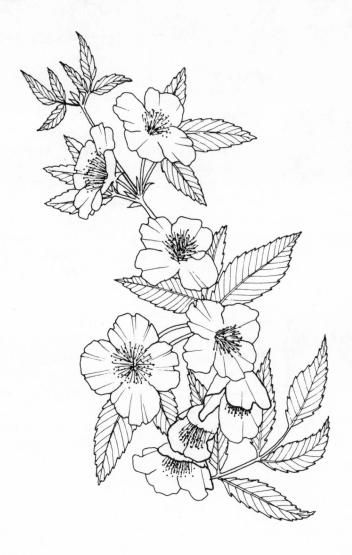

FRUIT

Prune

Indoors: Thin out and train peaches, nectarines and cherries. Pinch out shoots on melons one or two leaves beyond the point at which each fruit is forming.

Outdoors: Summer prune cordon, espalier and other trained apples, pears, plums and sweet cherries. Remove unwanted runners from strawberries. Cut out old raspberry canes after fruiting. Summer prune gooseberries and red currants.

Spray

Indoors: Watch for mildew on grape vines. If seen, improve ventilation and spray or dust with a suitable fungicide.

Outdoors: Apples, against scab. Use protective sprays for mildew, and for leaf-miner and other pests on gooseberries; also leaf spot and rust on black currants. Apply liquid derris to gooseberries to keep down aphids and caterpillars.

Miscellaneous

If you intend to make a new strawberry bed, layer a sufficient number of the strongest runners for that purpose. When well rooted, plant them out during showery weather. When outdoor tomatoes form their first truss of fruit, a 5 cm (2 inch) layer of rotted manure around the plants will help the roots.

Apples, pears, plums and cherries can be budded this month (as for roses excepting that the buds are inserted about 20 cm (8 inches) above soil level).

Plum branches showing signs of silver leaf fungus should be cut out and burned. The typical metallic silvering of the leaf should not be confused with mildew. Cover the wound with a canker paint.

VEGETABLES

Sow

In prepared beds, dwarf pea, dwarf bean, and endive, for cloching in early September. *Outdoors:* Beetroot, shorthorn carrots, coleworts, first sowings of spring and summer cabbage, and successional sowings of chicory, endive, mustard and cress, parsley, early peas, radishes, prickly spinach, and herbs such as chervil, dill and parsley, and salad onions.

Plant or transplant

Indoors: Move tomato plants to final pots or plant direct into greenhouse border. *Outdoors:* Leeks from March sowings, celery, broccoli, Brussels sprouts, cabbages, cauliflowers, kale.

Prune

Indoors: Keep taking off tomato sideshoots. Take off also side growths of cucumbers when they cease to bear. Pinch out growing points of runner beans when they reach the tops of their supports.

Outdoors: Cut heads of globe artichokes while the scales are plump. They will be right for eating and their removal will strengthen the plants.

Spray

Indoors: Tomato plants overhead with a fine mist of plain water to encourage a good set of fruit.

Outdoors: Bordeaux mixture or mancozeb sprayed on both sides of the foliage will help keep out potato blight. Overhead spraying with water is reputed to help runner beans to set pods.

Miscellaneous

Peas, marrow and French beans will now be cropping well and it is important to harvest them as they mature, otherwise the plants stop producing. If you are going on holiday, it is advisable to get a neighbour to gather mature crops so that plants do not cease bearing. Arrangements must be made for watering in the greenhouse.

When earthing up celery, do not let soil enter the hearts of the plants. Pull off any side-shoots which are seen. Shallots should be ready for lifting. First scrape soil away from the bulbs; then, after a couple of days, lift them carefully, laying them out to dry before storing them in a dry, airy place.

Herbs for winter use should be gathered. Cut them before they flower, and tie the stems in small bundles, suspending their heads downwards in a cool, dry, airy place, or they can be placed in the deep freezer and used later for flavouring.

In the vegetable garden, autumn sown onions will have completed their growth and ripened their bulbs. Lift them carefully and lay them in a sunny place to dry before storing.

FLOWERS

Sow
Indoors: Herbaceous calceolaria, carnation, cineraria, penstemon (in cold frame), primula.
Outdoors: Brompton stock, forget-me-not, hollyhock, pansy.

Plant or transplant
Indoors: Prick off and pot seedlings of calceolaria, cineraria and primula before they become crowded. Old cyclamen corms in pots. Re-pot primula and other plants

needing more room. Move winter-flowering begonias into 13–15 cm (5–6 inch) flower pots.

Outdoors: Colchicum, autumn-flowering crocus, *Lilium candidum*, sternbergia. Seedlings of biennials and perennials sown in early June. Divide and replant *Primula pulverulenta.*

Prune

Indoors: Hydrangea, to encourage next year's flowering growth. Chrysanthemum, pinch out top of late-rooted plants. Regal and fancy pelargoniums can be cut down and cuttings of the best varieties potted.

Outdoors: Cut back roses when flowers fade. Long branches of rambler roses should be cut to within a few inches of the ground. Shrubs that have just finished flowering or have flowered earlier, including deutzia, weigela and philadelphus.

Cuttings from evergreen hedges and flowering shrubs should now be taken if new stock is required.

Shorten young shoots of wisteria and tie in leading shoots.

Remove unwanted basal growths from chrysanthemums and dahlias.

Spray

Indoors: Cyclamen, with water, in the morning and evening during warm weather.

Greenhouse floor and staging, with water or pesticide, to keep down red spider mite and thrips.

Outdoors: Spray all parts of the flower garden with a good fungicide to prevent mildew, moulds, black spot, rust and botrytis from gaining a hold.

Miscellaneous

Various shrubs can be increased by cuttings of half-ripe shoots. These may be pulled off as 'slips' with a 'heel' of older wood or trimmed off cleanly. Root them in a frame or a fairly deep box covered with a sheet of glass. Border carnations can be propagated by pegging down shoots. Pinks and rock roses root easily from cuttings.

Clematis can be increased by layering, that is, pegging down shoots in pots of soil sunk into the ground.

The lawn may need feeding or weeding or both. In dry weather set the mower blades a notch higher than usual. When the foliage of bulbs grown in grass has died down, the mower can be taken over them.

July is the principle month for budding roses. It cannot be done satisfactorily unless the bark lifts easily from the wood. This it will not do during hot, dry weather.

Stems of young dahlia plants should be tied in and, once the plants are growing well, they can be fed with liquid fertilizer. If long-stemmed blooms are required, some disbudding is usually necessary.

Excepting the spray and pompon varieties, the number of shoots on chrysanthemum plants should be reduced to five.

Strong growing pinks sometimes burst their calyx. To prevent this on flowers wanted for exhibition purposes, there are special calyx bands which can be used. Ground over-rich in nitrogen encourages calyx splitting.

Take off faded flowers from pansies and violas.

CHAPTER TEN

August

While there is not much bustle in greenhouse or garden this month, there are some jobs which are essential to carry out to ensure next season's display of colour or a good weight of crops.

In the greenhouse, ventilation will be needed day and night unless conditions are unusual. Shading should be checked, for valued plants may still be at risk in strong, scorching sunshine. As the earliest batches of achimenes, begonias, gloxinias and hippeastrums pass out of flowering, their water supply should be reduced, to encourage them to rest.

Bulbs and corms to be potted this month include cyclamen, Roman hyacinth, lachenalia and narcissus – some of them to flower at Christmas. In the open ground, when rambler roses go out of flower they should be overhauled, the older stems being cut right back to their base so that the young growths are strengthened. Cuttings of both zonal and ivy-leaved geraniums (pelargoniums) and fuchsias can be taken this month. They root readily in pots or boxes of sandy compost.

Onions from sowings made early in the year will now be ripening. This process can often be hastened by scraping the soil from the bulbs and bending over the leaves.

If pansy, viola, aubrieta and similar plants are cut back, they will produce new growths suitable for cuttings.

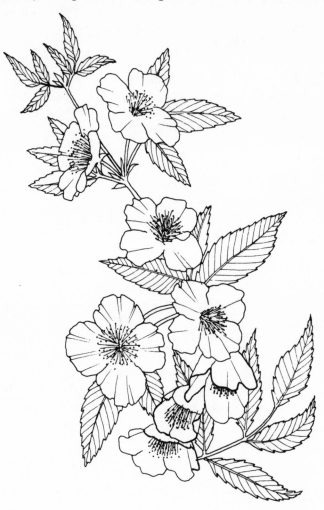

FRUIT

Plant or transplant
Outdoors: Well rooted strawberry runners, container-grown fruit trees and bushes.

Prune

Indoors: Trained cherries; removing shoots that have borne fruit.
Outdoors: Same as July; plus summer-fruiting raspberries; black currants, after fruiting. Remove dead wood and broken branches from plums and damsons; shorten side-shoots of gooseberries and red and white currants.

Spray

Indoors: During hot weather spray with water all pot-grown and trained fruit trees.
Outdoors: Spray stone fruit (after the middle of August) against bacterial canker. Spray gooseberries and currants with derris when fruit has been gathered. Brush methylated spirit into patches of woolly aphis. Treat acid cherries with a copper fungicide against canker.

Miscellaneous

Gather apples as they become ready. Early varieties can be picked when slightly under-ripe.

If the strawberry bed is to be retained for another year, it should be thoroughly cleaned after all fruit has been gathered. Take away all debris and unwanted runners, which should be severed close to the crown and not pulled off or part of the crown may be damaged. Unhealthy plants should be discarded and straw which surrounded the plants burned along with hibernating pests. After cleaning the bed, lightly fork over the soil between the rows, burying any manure applied in early spring.

Protection from birds should be given to ripening peaches and nectarines. Small-mesh netting fixed below the branches will catch falling fruit and prevent bruising.

VEGETABLES

Sow

Indoors: Cucumbers for fruiting in November and December.

Outdoors: Red cabbages, spring cabbages, endive, winter lettuce, onions, winter spinach. Sow mustard as a green mature crop on vacant ground.

Plant or transplant

Indoors: Young tomato plants for early winter fruiting.

Outdoors: Continue to plant broccoli, celery, leeks, kale, Savoys.

Prune

Indoors: Take out growing points of tomatoes as they become weaker and thin.

Spray

Indoors: Tomatoes against blight, lettuce against aphids, weevils and thrips.

Outdoors: Spray peas against thrips and use a fungicide against mildew. Continue to spray runner beans during evenings of hot days. Give a second spraying of Bordeaux mixture to potatoes.

Feed tomato plants now that they are in full bearing.

Miscellaneous

Runner beans and celery needing plenty of moisture and if the weather remains dry, both should be watered freely. Cucumbers, in frames and outdoors, will also need to be well fed and watered.

From the middle of this month, celery will need blanching. Do this gradually, drawing up the soil towards the stems, but first remove offsets or suckers.

From now on, there will be quite a lot of garden waste which should be placed on the compost heap. To encourage even decomposition as the heap is built, sprinkle each layer with a proprietory accelerator or sulphate of ammonia. Kitchen waste can be added to the heap, but not polythene or similar material.

Second early potatoes should be ready for lifting. It is best to let them lie in the open air for an hour or two, so that the skin becomes firm before they are placed in bags or boxes.

The earliest endive can now be blanched – a few plants at a time. A simple method is to cover each plant with an inverted flower pot with the hole covered to shut out the light. Up to fourteen days are needed for blanching.

Early beetroot should be lifted. Twist off the tops without injuring the skin and store them in a cool place. If surrounded by slightly moist sand they will keep well.

FLOWERS

Sow

Indoors: Celosia, cyclamen, busy lizzie (impatiens), winter-flowering stock, mignonette (for pots), streptocarpus.

Outdoors: Brompton stock, pansy, viola, freshly gathered seed of primula and the blue poppy (*Meconopis betonicifolia*).

Plant or transplant

Indoors: Move seedling calceolarias into 8 cm (3 inch) pots. Re-pot old cyclamen corms and arum lily. Prepared and Roman hyacinths, cyclamen, cineraria, calceolaria, freesia, lachenalia, winter-flowering begonia.

Outdoors: Plant out cuttings of pinks as soon as they are well rooted. Move biennial stocks to flowering quarters. Plant

Lilium candidum, *L. testaceum*, colchicum, autumn crocus, sternbergia, pyrethrum.

Prune

Indoors: Show and regal pelargoniums. Trim back *Campanula isophylla* using healthy growths for cuttings.

Outdoors: Evergreen shrubs and hedges, hydrangea. Remove faded flower spikes from dahlia, delphinium, sweet pea.

Thin growths of oxygenating plants in pools and ponds.

Shorten tips of young shoots of vigorous wisterias.

Spray

Indoors: Apply overhead watering to cyclamen. Feed exhibition chrysanthemums once flower buds are seen. Control aphids with a systemic insecticide.

Outdoors: Dahlias, roses, against pests, and inspect for virus infection. Gladiolus, to destroy thrips. *Lilium candidum* with systemic insecticide against aphids, and with fungicide against botrytis. Cuttings of alpines, with water.

Miscellaneous

The planting or replanting of bearded irises should be completed this month. Some of the bulbous species, such as *I. reticulata*, like early planting too. These should be examined closely since sometimes they are attacked by a fungus, seen as inky-black blotches which cause decay.

As cordon-trained sweet peas reach the tops of their supports, they should be untied and lowered. Lay the stems along the ground and retrain them up canes about 2 cm (6 ft) further along the row.

'Everlasting' flowers for drying will now need gathering. The flowers should be cut just before the petals are fully expanded, the stems being tied into bunches and hung upside down in a cool, airy place.

CHAPTER ELEVEN

September

The approach of autumn brings a temptation to reduce activity, but the temptation must be avoided for neglect of seasonal jobs would mean more work later.

As leaves begin to fall they should be collected and stacked or added to the compost heap. In the flower garden, the planting of bulbs and corms for spring flowering can now begin.

Throughout the month cuttings of a wide variety of items can be taken, including penstemon, geranium (zonal pelargonium), pansy, viola and verbena. Sometimes it is possible to pull non-flowering shoots from pansies and violas complete with roots. Violets can be removed to frames for winter flowering. A sunny situation where the soil is up to 20 cm (8 inches) deep is suitable.

Chrysanthemums to flower later in the greenhouse can now be taken inside. Give them plenty of room, to lessen risk of mildew.

FRUIT

Plant or transplant

Indoors: Figs are best grown in pots so that their roots can be confined, leading to better fruit production, and potting can be done now. Plunge the pots outdoors in sandy soil until December.

Outdoors: Strawberry runners. Prepare sites for planting fruit trees and bushes as well as wall specimens, working-in well rotted manure or compost.

Prune

Indoors: Trained trees which are tending to become too big or unshapely.

Outdoors: Complete summer pruning of apples, pears and morello cherries. Cut back and tie-in wall-trained peaches, nectarines and plums. Cut out old canes of blackberries and loganberries as fruiting finishes, and train-in new growths. Finish cutting out old raspberry canes.

Spray

Indoors: Where mildew is seen, spray with a fungicide, ventilate as a preventative,

86

and water carefully, chiefly early in the day so that foliage is dry by nightfall.
Outdoors: Spray apple and stone fruit with Bordeaux mixture if canker is suspected.

Miscellaneous
Grease-band fruit trees to catch insects, including the winter moth, crawling up the trunks. It is also possible to apply the grease directly on to the bark. If you order fruit trees this autumn consider cordons, since they bear heavily in proportion to the small space they occupy. They will grow against walls and fences, or as a hedge. Apart from apples and pears, red currants, gooseberries and plums do well as cordons or espaliers.

Apples and pears should be picked as soon as they part readily from the branches. Pears ripen quickly and are often past their best within a day or two. They should therefore be checked frequently.

Fallen apples suffering from brown rot should be gathered and burned, otherwise the disease will carry over to the following season.

Melons in the greenhouse will be finishing growth, but plants in frames will still be ripening their fruits, so the atmosphere must be kept dry. Less water at the roots will be needed – stop syringing.

VEGETABLES

Sow

Indoors: Dwarf French beans, cress, endive, lettuce, mustard, radishes.

Outdoors: Onions, winter spinach, Brussels sprouts, corn salad and cauliflowers for moving to frame later, and turnips for 'tops'. Hardy lettuce such as 'Dandie', 'Imperial' and 'Arctic King'. Sow carrot 'Early Market' under cloches; and parsley and chervil in a sheltered place.

Plant or transplant

Indoors: Parsley seedlings raised outdoors.

Outdoors: Continue to plant brassicas but leave room for August-sown plants; select a sheltered position for planting winter lettuce. Prick out cauliflower seedlings.

Prune

Indoors: Cucumbers, taking off all spent growths.

Outdoors: Pull off older leaves of spring-sown parsley to encourage a cluster of young leaves to develop. Cut off and burn all potato haulms affected by disease.

Spray

Indoors: Tomatoes, cucumbers and other vegetables showing signs of mildew.

Outdoors: Celery and outdoor tomatoes with liquid copper. Continue to spray cabbage against caterpillars and celery against the fly.

Miscellaneous

When cold weather threatens, bring green or partly-coloured tomatoes into warmth. Placed in a box of hay, wrapped in paper, or left in a drawer, they will ripen evenly.

Where a spare frame is available, an extra sowing of corn salad can be made now. Broadcast the seed thinly and cover it with half an inch of soil and gradually remove and use the largest seedlings so that the remaining plants are left 10–12 cm (4–5 inches) apart.

Prepare the site where lettuce seed is to be sown under cloches towards the end of the month. Ensure that drainage is good, since the plants will have to remain in position until next March or April. Cover July-sown peas with cloches.

Garden frames and lights should be cleaned and repaired. Warm soapy water with a dash of paraffin will help in the cleaning.

Yellowing asparagus foliage should be cleared before the berries ripen because if seedlings develop they will overcrowd the bed.

Where seeds of onions and leeks are

being saved, the mature heads should now be cut and placed in the greenhouse, or under a cloche or Dutch light, to finish ripening. Ventilate freely to prevent mildew.

When potatoes are lifted, damaged or diseased tubers should be cleared from the plot or they will encourage slugs.

FLOWERS

Sow

Indoors: Annuals for flowering in pots in the greenhouse, antirrhinum, new crop lilium seeds, schizanthus for spring display.

Outdoors: Sweet alyssum, calendula, candytuft, clarkia, cornflower, godetia, larkspur, nemophila, nigella, Shirley poppy, saponaria, annual scabious, viscaria.

Sow lawn grass seed on prepared sites.

Plant or transplant

Indoors: As August, plus cyclamen seedlings; and bulbs in pots and bowls, including daffodil (narcissus), freesia, hyacinth, iris, lachenalia, lily, tulip, veltheimia. Violets in frames. Tender bedding plants from outdoors. Pot up a few leaf-bud cuttings of camellias. Move strong polyanthus seedlings to pots for early flowering. *Outdoors:* Rooted carnation layers. Bulbs and corms including anemone, crocus, hardy cyclamen, daffodil (narcissus), iris, lilium, muscari, scilla, snowdrop and other spring-flowering bulbs. Herbaceous plants (not in flower). Evergreen shrubs and trees. Transplant biennials and perennials sown earlier.

Prune

Outdoors: Rambler roses (as soon as flowers fade). Trim laurel hedges. Pinch back unwanted wistaria growths. Cut off all dead flower heads to prolong display.

Spray

Indoors: Cyclamen in frames, using clear water overhead, night and morning. Late chrysanthemums in pots, using a combined insecticide and fungicide, before taking them under glass.
Outdoors: Chrysanthemum, delphinium, roses, Michaelmas daisy and any other subjects showing signs of mildew.

Miscellaneous

Border carnations layered last month will now be well rooted and ready for moving to their flowering positions.

Several species of hardy primula, if

left to themselves, soon become crowded, with fewer flowers. These include polyanthus, *Primula auricula, P. denticulata, P. winteri* and *P. florindae*. All can be divided this month.

Cuttings of lavender taken now will root readily in a sheltered place outdoors. Silver sand sprinkled into the bottom of the hole will encourage good rooting.

Many perennials are apt to look untidy at this time of year. Keep faded flowers removed and the stems well supported, so that they do not flop about. This also applies to dahlias, which will need some disbudding and thinning out of basal shoots.

This is a good time to transplant evergreen shrubs, of which cuttings can also be taken. They will root well in a frame or sheltered position. Make them about 15 cm (6 inches) long and if possible take them with a 'heel' of old wood. Aucuba, laurel, lavender, lonicera, privet and rosemary are all suitable for this treatment.

Lawn grass seed can be sown when the soil is moist. On well-prepared sites sow 42–57 gm ($1\frac{1}{2}$ –2 oz) to the sq m (sq yd).

CHAPTER TWELVE

October

Shortening days and falling temperatures bring many attractive changes in the colour of the landscape. Fallen leaves should be swept up and added to the compost heap with plant refuse such as old bean and pea haulms, carrot and beetroot tops, and cabbage and lettuce leaves.

It is time to take the last of the half-hardy plants under cover.

Tidy up the herbaceous border. Lift and divide crowded plants, retaining the more vigorous outer parts (leave autumn-flowering plants until spring).

All vacant plots should be dug over. Farmyard manure, compost, leaf mould, or peat laced with bone meal, should be dug in.

Plant deciduous trees and shrubs just after leaf-fall. In colder areas, do not move the more tender shrubs until late spring.

FRUIT

Plant or transplant
Indoors: Figs, peaches, nectarines.
Outdoors: Late strawberry plants, raspberry canes and (after leaf-fall) apples, pears and plums.

Prune
Indoors: Apricots and figs.
Outdoors: Blackberries, red and white currants, gooseberries, loganberries. Root-prune apples, plums and pears if essential. Remove unwanted runners from strawberries. Remove badly placed and dead branches on old apple, pear and cherry trees and bushes.

Spray
Indoors: Peaches and nectarines at leaf-fall with a fungicide, against leaf curl.
Outdoors: Peaches and nectarines (same treatment as those indoors). Apple trees showing signs of canker also need a copper spray just before leaf-fall. Spray cherries against bacterial canker.

Miscellaneous

In this great harvesting month, select only sound fruits for storage. Fruits should not be piled one on top of another but, wherever possible, laid out on single-layer trays. Apples keep best in a slightly moist atmosphere – pears like rather drier conditions.

Prepare and enrich the sites in advance where fruit trees are to be planted.

When choosing fruit trees, take care to select self-fertile varieties or plant suitable pollinators.

Established stone fruit trees such as plums, damsons and cherries, which have grown too rampantly, can be root-pruned. A dressing of lime on the soil around the trees will prove beneficial.

VEGETABLES

Sow

Indoors: Lettuce, mustard and cress, radishes.

Outdoors: Dwarf peas (in sheltered border), corn salad, spinach, parsley, endive.

Plant or transplant
Indoors: Box or pot mint for forcing, rhubarb, parsley, cauliflowers; chicory for forcing; spring cabbage.
Outdoors: Spring cabbage, coleworts, winter lettuce, endive.

Prune
Outdoors: Cut down asparagus to near ground level.

Spray

Indoors: Any crops including brassicas still in the ground showing signs of mildew or fungus spots.
Outdoors: The base of hedges and fences where pests and disease spores often find shelter.

Miscellaneous
Take care of plants in the cold frame by closing the lights on very cold days and leaving them off on fine, mild ones. As a precaution against botrytis, dust all plants in frames and cloches with a fungicide powder.

Potatoes in frost-proof sheds or cellars should be examined at regular intervals. Remove any showing any signs of disease.

Maturing cauliflowers can be protected from frost damage by breaking inwards a leaf or two. Remove dead or yellowing leaves from all brassica plants.

Clear weeds and rubbish from asparagus and rhubarb and apply a good mulching of manure to build up next season's crowns.

Overgrown Savoys can be encouraged to heart-up by prising them up carefully to break the tap roots and then treading them back firmly into place.

Horseradish can become a nuisance if allowed to spread. This is a good time to dig it up. The large roots can be stored in damp sand or ashes for winter use, and the thinner ones prepared for replanting in March. Cut them into lengths of 23 cm (9 inches) with a slant at the bottom. Then tie in bunches and store in sandy soil until planting time.

FLOWERS

Sow
Indoors: Alpines, antirrhinum, stock, sweet pea.
Outdoors: Sweet pea.

Plant or transplant
Indoors: Hardy plants, bulbs, calceolaria, cineraria, streptocarpus, primula, green-

house shrubs and climbers. Dutch and Spanish irises, ixias, *Azalea indica*, lilies for forcing, arum lilies.

Outdoors: Border carnations, hardy perennials, biennials, spring bedding plants, including double daisy, forget-me-not, polyanthus and wallflower, lily of the valley, hyacinth, tulip and other hardy bulbs, evergreen shrubs and trees, roses.

Prune

Indoors: Take off unwanted flower buds from chrysanthemums and perpetual-flowering carnations.

Outdoors: Rambler roses, deciduous climbing plants. Cut down dahlias when frost has blackened foliage. Lift and divide rampant rock-plants such as saxifrages and sedums, replanting small, rooted pieces.

Spray

Indoors: Chrysanthemums against mildew, carnations.

Outdoors: Continue spraying roses against greenfly and fungus diseases.

Miscellaneous

As soon as the summer flower beds have been cleared of begonia, dahlia, geranium, lobelia, salvia and other bedders, prepare the soil and start planting spring-flowering subjects. These include double daisy, forget-me-not, polyanthus, wallflower and Siberian wallflower (*Cheiranthus allionii*). These plants can be used also as groundwork for April and May flowering tulips, the bulbs of which can be planted at the same time as the plants. No special preparation is necessary but a good sprinkling of bonemeal, lightly forked in, will help to improve the soil.

Many popular herbaceous perennials can be divided, but on heavy ground it may be better to wait until early spring. Subjects include aquilegia, delphinium, iris, lychnis, phlox and Shasta daisy (*Chrysanthemum maximum*). *Lobelia cardinalis* can be divided but must be kept in pots in warmth for the winter.

A good lawn improves the look of the flower garden, and there is still time to sow seed, but germination will be slow. Alternatively, turf can be laid and it will have time to settle before winter. The site should be free from weeds, and enriched with a good fertilizer. Good turf is usually supplied in the size 30 cm (1 ft) by 90 cm (3 ft) and should be of uniform thickness. Lay the turves in staggered rows, like brickwork, fitting them closely together and filling any depressions with fine soil. Take out weeds as soon as they are seen during the next few months.

CHAPTER THIRTEEN

November

There is much that can be done this month when weather permits, and since the days are short it is essential to make the most of them. Planting of herbaceous perennials can be done when the soil is workable. Some, such as anchusa, anthemis, coreopsis, delphinium and gaillardia, should not be moved after the last week in this month. Their roots are quite fleshy and are vulnerable to severe cold or wet weather. *Scabiosa caucasica* and *Aster amellus* are best moved in the spring.

Established herbaceous borders should be cleaned up, old stems being cut down and weeds removed. When outdoor chrysanthemums finish flowering they should be cut down; a few roots can be moved to a vacant frame and used later for cuttings.

Where choice alpine or rock garden plants are being grown, any of doubtful hardiness can be given the protection of a bell glass, cloche or even a sheet of glass. Place these so that there is free circulation of air.

There are both tender and hardy cyclamen, and the former will soon be in great demand as pot plants for Christmas. The earliest of the hardy sorts will now be passing over, but there are others which will show colour from January to April.

Planting of bulbs for spring flowering is an important job this month.

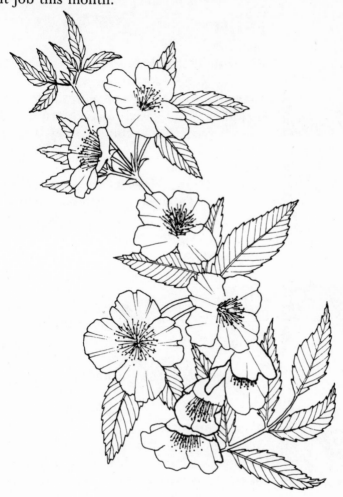

FRUIT

Plant or transplant
Indoors: Renew soil of pot fruits.
Outdoors: Apples, pears, plums, soft fruits including cultivated blackberries, and loganberries (but excluding strawberries).

Prune
Indoors: Grape vines as soon as they are dormant. Thin out superfluous shoots of figs. Shorten leading apricot shoots.
Outdoors: Apples, pears, red currants and gooseberries.

Spray
Indoors: Fan trained apricots, peaches, nectarines, trained and bush apples and plums.
Outdoors: Apples, pears, plums, peaches, cherries, soft fruit, using tar oil winter wash.

Miscellaneous
When pruning fruit trees watch for damage caused by branches rubbing together, or by pests. Apple canker may enter such

wounds unless the wounds are cleaned and treated with canker paint.

Dessert pears in store must be used immediately they are ripe or they will go sleepy and useless.

Cuttings of gooseberries and black and red currants can be taken in the same way as shrubs. Gooseberries should be grown in a 'leg' and all but the three top buds should be rubbed out before putting the cuttings in the ground.

VEGETABLES

Sow
Indoors: Dwarf beans, lettuce, mustard and cress, radishes, cauliflowers 'All the Year Round' (sown in pots).
Outdoors: Longpod broad beans and round-seeded dwarf peas.

Plant or transplant
Indoors: Pot or box rhubarb and seakale for forcing. Thin winter lettuce.
Outdoors: Cabbages, leeks, Savoys.

Spray

Indoors: Lettuce and late tomatoes against greenfly.

Outdoors: Apply Bordeaux mixture or a similar fungicide to the soil around Brussels sprouts, cabbages and other brassicas.

Miscellaneous

Cloches can be kept on autumn-sown Brussels sprouts and lettuce. Take off the lower open rosettes at the base of Brussels sprout stems, for they will never button up. Also remove the yellow leaves from all brassicas.

Tubers of Chinese artichokes can be lifted now and stored in boxes or trays of moist sand in a frost-proof place where they will be available as required.

Put another casing of soil on the potato clamp, giving extra protection to the base. Have material available as additional cover for tubers being stored in sheds and cellar, during spells of severe frosts.

In light, well-drained soil and unexposed places, there is still time to sow corn salad.

Complete winter digging as soon as possible. On medium and heavy land, manure can be dug in at the same time, but on light soil, it may be better to add this in the spring.

If weather remains mild, leeks may benefit from applications of liquid manure.

Don't rush to use kale at this time, for

it is much more palatable after it has been subjected to fairly severe frosts.

Heel over towards the north plants of late cauliflower. To do this, dig plants from the soil on the north side, pulling the stems down and then replacing the soil.

FLOWERS

Sow

Indoors: Cyclamen for next autumn, *Grevillea robusta*.

Outdoors: Collect berries of ornamental shrubs including holly for stratification in preparation for sowing next year. Store them in sand, and bury them for at least six months, after which they will germinate freely.

Plant or transplant

Indoors: Azalea, hydrangea, lilac and other shrubs for forcing. Astilbe, Christmas rose, dicentra and polyanthus. Prick out and pot late seedlings; plant bulbs in pots.

Outdoors: Herbaceous plants, hardy bulbs, deciduous shrubs and trees. Climbing plants (including roses), heather, tulip and other bulbs. Anemone, lily of the valley, ranunculus and spring-flowering bedding plants. Use compact varieties when planting shrubs in containers for garden and patio decoration.

Prune
Indoors: Climbing plants, to prevent too much shade later. Prune roots of roses being potted for forcing. Pinch out shoots of winter cherry (solanum) which are hiding the berries.
Outdoors: Deciduous hardy hedging plants; climbing and wall plants. Complete cutting back of alpine plants. Cut back both garden and greenhouse chrysanthemums that have finished flowering.

Spray
Indoors: Occasional overhead syringings of water applied early in the day will prove beneficial. Use malathion spray on plants susceptible to leaf miner. Spray or fumigate against whitefly and aphids.
Outdoors: Evergreen and deciduous hedges suspected of harbouring aphids. Use a derris or pyrethrum solution.

Miscellaneous
Shorter days and longer evenings mean that we can begin armchair gardening this month – planning for next season.

Good gardening days being rare now, we must take full advantage of them. Planting of all ornamental subjects should continue. Make sure the roots of roses and shrubs are quite moist before they go into the ground. Damaged roots and twiggy shoots should be cut off. Surround the roots with moist peat and a sprinkling of bonemeal before firming the soil.

Dahlia tubers, chrysanthemums and other plants being given protection for the winter will need to be examined occasionally. If dahlia roots show signs of shrivelling, soak them in tepid water for a few hours.

Gladiolus corms should also be checked and any diseased specimens discarded. If there was an attack of thrips during the growing season, dust the corms with malathion.

Many alpine plants will benefit from a general trim, and where rains have washed soil from the plants it should be replaced. Shingle or stone chippings on the surface will help to suppress weeds.

Check the stakes and ties of newly planted standard trees. Tread the soil around the roots if they are loosened by frosts.

CHAPTER FOURTEEN

December

With so much to do and so little good daylight time, there is a temptation to plant when the soil is wet and sticky. It is better to wait.

Autumn-sown sweet peas in frames may need extra attention during severe frosts. Rapid thawing can kill the seedlings. If any do become frozen, spray them with *cold* water so that they thaw gradually.

Check bulbs, corms, and tubers in store, including potatoes and other root crops, for signs of rot or mildew.

Protect outdoor taps and water pipes.

This is a month when many people receive pot plants as gifts, especially at Christmas, and yet it is the most difficult time to keep plants because the days are short and the light is poor. It is a mistake to think that heat can take the place of light and to place plants in the darkest part of the room to get them near to a fire or radiator – which they do not like. Overwatering is a common fault and many plants are killed by kindness. Generally it is wrong to give plants a little water every day in winter. It is better to let the soil get near dry and then water well. But remember that plants need much less water in winter than in summer.

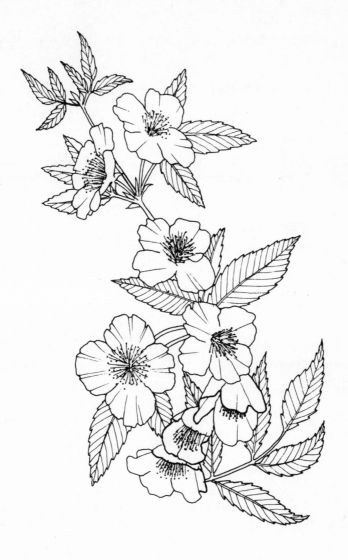

FRUIT

Plant or transplant
Indoors: Apple, pear, apricot, peach, nectarine and grape vines, for borders or pots.
Outdoors: As November, when weather and soil are favourable.

Prune
Indoors: Finish pruning grape vines, lowering rods to check flow of sap. Thin shoots of exhibition gooseberries. Prune peach, nectarine, apricots.
Outdoors: Continue pruning trees and bushes when weather is mild.

Spray
Indoors: Dormant trees and bushes.
Outdoors: Give first application of tar oil winter wash to dormant fruit trees, bushes and cane fruits.

Miscellaneous
The best supports for fruit trees growing on walls are horizontal wires, 30 cm (12 inches) apart and 8–10 cm (3–4 inches) from the walls. These can be tied con-

veniently now while growth is dormant.

Morello cherries are particularly suitable for growing on a north-facing wall. They are hardy and self-fertile.

If you are planting new raspberry canes, prepare the ground well by trenching it 60 cm (2 ft) deep and adding a good layer of manure or compost.

Where birds are troublesome, it is unwise to prune gooseberries and red currants until late January. Delay prevents the birds from spoiling the new buds. Strands of black cotton placed over the bushes in a zig-zag manner help to keep off sparrows.

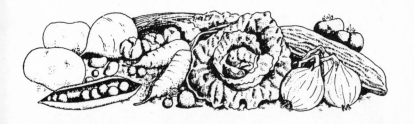

VEGETABLES

Sow
Indoors: Where heating is adequate, sow a few tomatoes for a very early picking. Sow also carrots, salad onions, mustard and cress, dwarf beans for forcing.
Outdoors: Broad beans and shallots, in light, well drained soils.

111

Plant or transplant

Indoors: Transplant lettuce from October sowings. Force more rhubarb. Box chicory and place in a temperature of 12°C (55°F). Plant out cauliflowers in cold house.

Outdoors: Potatoes and onions when soil is workable.

Prune

Indoors: Remove all diseased and discoloured leaves from plants.

Outdoors: Take off yellowing and dead leaves from brassica plants.

Spray

Indoors: A general insecticide or fumigant will destroy pests hidden in crevices.

Outdoors: Autumn-sown lettuce, peas and beans if mildew is seen. Use slug killer around herb bed.

Miscellaneous

Cold frames must be ventilated regularly; damp, stagnant air encourages fungus diseases.

Longpod broad bean seedlings from October and November sowings should be given protection by drawing up the soil on both sides of the rows. Although quite hardy, they should be spared prolonged spells of severe weather.

Clear ground where crops are finished, and put all healthy material on the compost heap. If extra greenstuff is likely to be wanted in the spring, the stumps of freshly-cut healthy cabbage can be left in the ground, two cross cuts being made on the stumps to encourage production of green shoots later.

FLOWERS

Sow
Indoors: Shrubs and climbers including clematis, cotoneaster.

Plant or transplant
Indoors: Retarded lily of the valley.
Outdoors: Hardy herbaceous plants. Arabis, Canterbury bell, double daisy, forget-me-not, foxglove, late tulip, climbing plants, deciduous shrubs.

Prune
Indoors: Lightly prune climbing roses, removing old worn shoots. Remove growing points when sweet pea seedlings are about 5 cm (2 inches) tall. Cut back chrysanthemums as they finish flowering.
Outdoors: Cut down all perennial plants out of flower. Cut back secondary shoots of

winter jasmine to 30 cm (12 inches) from the base. Also prune *Clematis jackmannii*, deciduous hedges, hardy fuchsia and deciduous ceanothus, and willow grown for its ornamental bark.

Spray

Indoors: On bright days ferns benefit from overhead syringing with plain water. Use Nimrod T to conrol rust and leaf spot on carnations and pinks. Fumigate if greenfly is seen.

Outdoors: Remains of mildewed Michaelmas daisies. Spray azalea and rhododendron buds with a bird deterrent.

Miscellaneous

Foremost among outdoor flowering plants at this time of the year is the Christmas Rose (*Helleborus niger*). If the plants are near a south-facing wall and are given some kind of glass protection, they really do flower for Christmas. Shoots can be cut from winter-flowering subjects such as winter jasmine, *Viburnum tinus*, *Prunus subhirtella*, and others, when they are in bud. If these are brought indoors, the flowers will gradually open.

When water lodges round the necks of plants and becomes frozen, it causes damage. This applies to many rock garden plants. To avoid harm, clear away loose leaves and surround the plants with granite chippings.

Whenever weather and soil conditions

are favourable press on with the planting of roses, shrubs and trees. Evergreens of course are best moved in the spring or autumn.

If plants or trees arrive from the nursery when planting is impossible, they can be left in the bundle for a couple of days but after that they should be undone and heeled in. Properly heeled in (that is, planted temporarily) they can wait till conditions are right for permanent planting.

Gardening Notes

FRUIT

Sow

Plant or transplant

Prune

Spray

Miscellaneous

VEGETABLES

Sow

Plant or transplant

Prune

Spray

Miscellaneous

FLOWERS

Sow

Plant or transplant

Prune

Spray

Miscellaneous

FRUIT
Sow

Plant or transplant

Prune

Spray

Miscellaneous

VEGETABLES
Sow

Plant or transplant

Prune

Spray

Miscellaneous

FLOWERS
Sow

Plant or transplant

Prune

Spray

Miscellaneous

FRUIT

Sow

Plant or transplant

Prune

Spray

Miscellaneous

VEGETABLES

Sow

Plant or transplant

Prune

Spray

Miscellaneous

FLOWERS

Sow

Plant or transplant

Prune

Spray

Miscellaneous

FRUIT

Sow

Plant or transplant

Prune

Spray

Miscellaneous

VEGETABLES

Sow

Plant or transplant

Prune

Spray

Miscellaneous

FLOWERS

Sow

Plant or transplant

Prune

Spray

Miscellaneous

FRUIT

Sow

Plant or transplant

Prune

Spray

Miscellaneous

VEGETABLES

Sow

Plant or transplant

Prune

Spray

Miscellaneous

FLOWERS

Sow

Plant or transplant

Prune

Spray

Miscellaneous

JUNE

FRUIT
Sow

Plant or transplant

Prune

Spray

Miscellaneous

VEGETABLES
Sow

Plant or transplant

Prune

Spray

Miscellaneous

FLOWERS
Sow

Plant or transplant

Prune

Spray

Miscellaneous

121

FRUIT

Sow

Plant or transplant

Prune

Spray

Miscellaneous

VEGETABLES

Sow

Plant or transplant

Prune

Spray

Miscellaneous

FLOWERS

Sow

Plant or transplant

Prune

Spray

Miscellaneous

FRUIT
Sow

Plant or transplant

Prune

Spray

Miscellaneous

VEGETABLES
Sow

Plant or transplant

Prune

Spray

Miscellaneous

FLOWERS
Sow

Plant or transplant

Prune

Spray

Miscellaneous

FRUIT

Sow

Plant or transplant

Prune

Spray

Miscellaneous

VEGETABLES

Sow

Plant or transplant

Prune

Spray

Miscellaneous

FLOWERS

Sow

Plant or transplant

Prune

Spray

Miscellaneous

FRUIT

Sow

Plant or transplant

Prune

Spray

Miscellaneous

VEGETABLES

Sow

Plant or transplant

Prune

Spray

Miscellaneous

FLOWERS

Sow

Plant or transplant

Prune

Spray

Miscellaneous

FRUIT

Sow

Plant or transplant

Prune

Spray

Miscellaneous

VEGETABLES

Sow

Plant or transplant

Prune

Spray

Miscellaneous

FLOWERS

Sow

Plant or transplant

Prune

Spray

Miscellaneous

DECEMBER

FRUIT

Sow

Plant or transplant

Prune

Spray

Miscellaneous

VEGETABLES

Sow

Plant or transplant

Prune

Spray

Miscellaneous

FLOWERS

Sow

Plant or transplant

Prune

Spray

Miscellaneous